FOL
4-

D0906284

POCKET GUIDE TO ANCIENT
EGYPTIAN
HIEROGLYPHS

How to read and write Ancient Egyptian

RICHARD PARKINSON

THE BRITISH MUSEUM PRESS

For Gabriel

© 2003 Richard Parkinson

First published in 2003 by The British Museum Press

A division of The British Museum Company Ltd

38 Russell Square, London WC1B 3QQ

Reprinted 2004, 2005

ISBN 0 7141 3007 9

A catalogue record for this book is available from the British Library

Richard Parkinson has asserted the right to be identified as the author of this work.

Designed and typeset by Crayon Design

Printed in Italy by L.E.G.O. Spa

Front cover image: Detail of a wall-painting in the tomb of Horemheb showing the king offering to the goddess Hathor, about 1319–1292 BC. (Werner Forman Archive, E. Strouhal)

Acknowledgements

All the hieroglyphs were drawn by the author.

All the photographs were taken by the British Museum Photography and Imaging Service, © The Trustees of the British Museum except for those listed below.

Belgin Elbs, p. 83; Griffith Institute, Oxford, p. 53; Red-Head, p. 71, Susanne Woodhouse, p. 8 (top); Richard Parkinson pp. 6, 9 (top), 41, 47, 52, 55, 58, 65, 73, 77, 78, 80, 84, 90. The author's photographs were taken while lecturing on Bales Worldwide Nile cruises, and he is greatly indebted to Mrs Molly Bales for enabling him to return to Egypt. The text and concept owes much to Tim Reid and Carolyn Jones.

CONTENTS

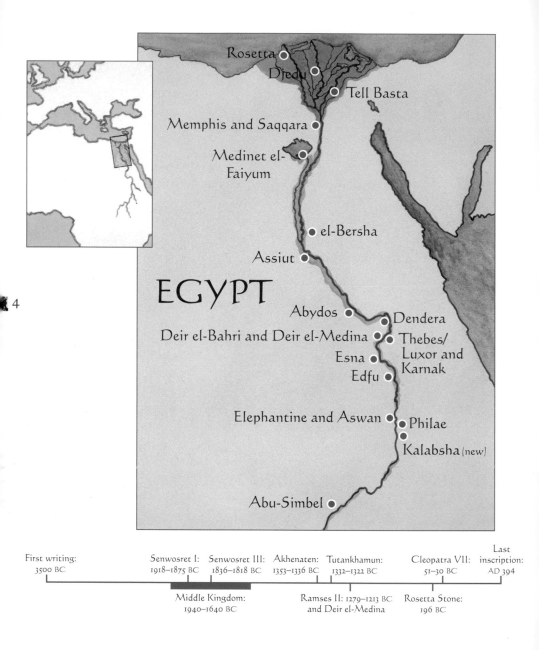

Rosetta

Djedu

Tell Basta

Memphis and Saqqara

Medinet el-
Faiyum

el-Bersha

Assiut

EGYPT

4

Abydos

Dendera

Deir el-Bahri and Deir el-Medina

Thebes/
Luxor and
Karnak

Esna

Edfu

Elephantine and Aswan

Philae

Kalabsha (new)

Abu-Simbel

First writing:
3500 BC

Senwosret I:
1918–1875 BC

Senwosret III:
1836–1818 BC

Akhenaten:
1353–1336 BC

Tutankhamun:
1332–1322 BC

Cleopatra VII:
51–30 BC

Last
inscription:
AD 394

Middle Kingdom:
1940–1640 BC

Ramses II: 1279–1213 BC
and Deir el-Medina

Rosetta Stone:
196 BC

1. Introduction

The ancient Egyptians wrote with signs that we now call hieroglyphs. This book will tell you a little about them and how to read them. It will show you how to read some Egyptian words, and explain how to write in the hieroglyphic script. The ancient Egyptians used about 750 hieroglyphic signs during the Middle Kingdom (1940–1640 BC) – you won't find all of them in this book. But you will discover how to read some of the most common and useful signs and words, the ones that you'll often see on Egyptian objects in books and in museums. Many of the signs shown here are from objects now in the British Museum. Others come from sites in Egypt, or from objects now in other museums.

An Ancient Mystery

The word 'hieroglyph' is Greek, and it means 'sacred carving'. The name was given to the hieroglyphic script by ancient Greek visitors to Egypt around the fifth century BC. The hieroglyphic script was used continuously in Egypt for almost four thousand years – much longer than our alphabet has been used. The ancient Greeks and Romans were fascinated by hieroglyphs because they looked so different from their own writing. The Roman Emperor Hadrian even had an obelisk made and carved with hieroglyphs for his friend Antinous, who drowned in Egypt in AD 130.

The latest known hieroglyphic inscription, in the Gateway of Hadrian, Philae.

When Egypt became a Christian country and people stopped worshipping the ancient Egyptian gods, the Egyptians stopped using hieroglyphs as well. The latest hieroglyphic inscription with a date was carved on a temple gateway on the holy island of Philae. It was carved there by a priest of the goddess Isis, who was called Nesmeterakhemon. The inscription is dated AD 24 August 394. It was carved beside an image of the god Mandulis, which was later chipped away by the Christians.

Time passed. No one left any books explaining how to read the hieroglyphs, and gradually the ancient Egyptian language died out. It was replaced by Coptic and Arabic. At last all understanding of

Ancient Egyptian and the hieroglyphic writing system was lost. By the time of the European Renaissance in the fifteenth century AD, people believed that the signs were pictures which recorded secret ideas through symbols. So they made up all sorts of complicated explanations and meanings for the signs. If you saw a sign showing an owl , you might guess that it meant something to do with a bird. Some Greek and Renaissance scholars made it much more complicated. They said that it meant 'death'. That was because the owl catches its prey in the night suddenly, just as death comes suddenly to someone. In fact, as you'll soon see, the owl sign simply writes the letter 'm'!

The fact that each hieroglyphic sign was a picture, very different from the alphabetic scripts used by Mediterranean and European cultures, made the inscriptions look very mysterious. People in Europe already thought of Egypt as an exotic, old and wise culture, and so everyone desperately wanted to know what mysteries the hieroglyphs concealed.

Who Wrote Hieroglyphs?

The Egyptians themselves were partly to blame for this mystery. By the time the Greeks and Romans visited Egypt, the Egyptian scribes and priests were playing clever games with the hieroglyphic script. One good example is a hymn to the crocodile god Sobek-Ra written on the wall of his temple at Esna in southern Egypt.

The hymn is written out with hieroglyphs in such a way that each hieroglyph includes a picture of a crocodile. The writers were rather too clever, in fact, because this inscription is almost too difficult to read. It is not surprising that the Greeks and Romans thought that hieroglyphs must be pictures of ideas, or symbols, not simply letters that spelled out words.

For most of ancient Egyptian history, only one in a hundred people could read and write, so even in ancient Egypt hieroglyphs were a mystery to most people. Hieroglyphs could be seen on everything owned or built by the rich – temple walls, house doorways, furniture, papyri (a sort of paper made from Nile reeds) and even pots – but almost nobody else could read them.

A hymn to Sobek-Ra in his temple at Esna.

A painting of two scribes writing records of a harvest, from a tomb-chapel at Thebes.

If you learned to read and write in ancient Egypt, you were being trained to help in the government of the country. It also meant that you were a man – women did not usually learn to write. These trained writers were called 'scribes'. You can see them in many Egyptian carvings and paintings, sitting cross-legged and writing on papyrus rolls that they hold across their laps. The painting opposite comes from Thebes, from the tomb-chapel of a scribe called Menna from around 1360 BC. Scribes and officials used the hieroglyphic script to write down everything that was needed to run the country and also to record its culture carefully. Hieroglyphic writing is not necessarily about the mysteries of the universe – it is just as likely to be a laundry list, a letter or a poem!

Cracking the Code

For centuries scholars puzzled over hieroglyphs, but nobody had any success in deciphering them. Then in AD 1799 the Rosetta Stone was discovered. This stone carried an inscription with the same text in three different scripts. These were ancient Greek, which many scholars could read, hieroglyphs, and another kind of Egyptian writing called Demotic. By using the Rosetta Stone and other texts, a young French scholar named Jean-François Champollion realized in AD 1824 that hieroglyphs might be letters that spelled out the Egyptian language. He had learned Coptic, the language of the Egyptian Christians, which he guessed (correctly) had descended from Ancient Egyptian. Using this, and his knowledge of signs, he could start to read hieroglyphs.

hieroglyphs

Demotic

Greek

The Rosetta Stone is a fragment of a temple stela (inscribed slab) with a text in three scripts.

2. Hieroglyphic Signs

Recording a Language

The ancient Egyptian language was different from the languages which people speak in Europe and America today. For example, look at this English sentence:

THE CAT **SAT** ON THE MAT.

We put the subject first (the cat), then the verb (sat). But the ancient Egyptians put the verb first, followed by the subject, so they would write:

SAT THE CAT ON THE MAT

A **verb** is the word that tells us about the main action or condition in a sentence, such as 'make', 'run', 'do', 'is'.

The **subject** is the main thing which is acting, doing or being in a sentence.

Ancient Egyptian is quite different from Arabic, which is the language spoken in modern Egypt, although they come from the same family of languages. That family of languages spread geographically over northern Africa, the eastern Mediterranean, and western Asia.

Sound Signs

Here's a simple fact that nobody knew for hundreds of years after the end of the ancient Egyptian civilization: most of the hieroglyphic signs that you see in inscriptions are simple sound signs. (Remember the owl that writes the letter 'm'?) Hieroglyphs record the sounds of the Egyptian language – but only the consonants, not the vowels (a, e, i, o, and u). Reading something written without vowels is not as hard as it sounds. If you are good at texting, you should find it easy:

'Try rdng ths, fr xmpl. Nt vry hrd.'

> The sounds of the letters of the alphabet are divided into two groups. The letters where the air you breathe out as you speak isn't stopped by your tongue or lips at all are called 'vowels' (in English they are a, e, i, o, u).
> The other letters are the 'consonants'.

Different languages need slightly different alphabets, because they have different sounds. There are twenty-four written sounds in the Egyptian language, but these do not quite match the sounds written by our Western alphabet. Today we use the Roman alphabet, with some special accents (such as è and ê in French and ü in German).

Egyptologists use an alphabet devised by nineteenth-century scholars in order to 'transliterate' hieroglyphs out of pictures into letters.

Transliterate or translate?

To **transliterate** means to copy a text into a version of our alphabet, or one like ours. We can transliterate hieroglyphs into our own letters.

To **translate** means to put what the text says into our own language. We can translate Ancient Egyptian into English words, just as we can translate French into English.

You can see the transliteration alphabet on pages 14–16. It has some signs which are used to transliterate other Near Eastern languages as well. This is a useful reminder that Ancient Egyptian was very different from our languages, and also that we don't know exactly what the language sounded like. (To find out how these signs got their sounds, see page 21.)

Rough sound value	Transliteration	Sign	What the sign shows
glottal stop (sounds a bit like the sound in the middle of the word 'bottle' if you say it with a Cockney accent)	ꜣ		Egyptian vulture
y (as in 'yoke')	j		reed
y	jj, y		two reeds
y	jj, y		two short strokes (an abbreviated way of writing **y**!)
gutteral sound (Arabic ayin – sounds a bit like someone choking!)	ꜥ		forearm
w (as in 'ew' or 'u')	w		quail chick
w	w		curly stroke (an abbreviated way of writing **w**!)
b	b		foot
p	p		stool (?)

Rough sound value	Transliteration	Sign	What the sign shows
f	f		horned viper
m	m		owl
n	n		water
r	r		mouth
h (as in 'he')	h		reed shelter
emphatic h	$ḥ$		twisted wick
ch	$ḫ$		nobody is sure what this is!
kh	$ẖ$		animal's belly
z	z		door-bolt
s	s		folded cloth
sh (as in 'she')	$š$		pool
q (as in 'queen')	q		hill-slope
k	k		basket

Rough sound value	Transliteration	Sign	What the sign shows
g (as in 'gap')	*g*		stand for a jar
t	*t*		loaf of bread
ch (as in 'choke')	*ṯ*		rope tether
d	*d*		hand
j (as in 'joke')	*ḏ*		snake

Because the Egyptians did not write vowels, we usually just add an 'e' when needed to make the words easier to say. So you should pronounce *ḥtp* as 'hetep', but we don't know if this is how ancient Egyptians said it.

If there were just twenty-four signs, reading hieroglyphs would be quite easy. But things are a bit more complicated. As well as these alphabetic signs, there are signs that write groups of two and three consonants. On page 17 you can see some two-letter signs.

Sign	Transliteration	Rough sound value	What the sign shows
	ꜣw	aw	part of a backbone
	ꜣb	ab	chisel
	jr	ir	eye
	ꜥꜣ	aa	wooden column
	wr	wer	swallow
	mj	mi	milk jug in a net
	mn	men	gaming board with pieces on it
	mr	mer	hoe
	ms	mes	apron of foxes' skins
	nb	neb	basket
	kꜣ	ka	pair of arms
	tj	ti	pestle for grinding
	dj	di	arm holding a loaf

Some common three-letter signs are:

Sign	Transliteration	Rough sound value	What the sign shows
♀	ꜥnḫ	ankh	sandal-strap (often writes the phrase 'to be alive' and related words)
	wsr	weser	head and neck of a dog (often writes the word 'powerful' and related words)
	nfr	nefer	animal's heart and throat (often writes the words 'good' or 'beautiful' and related words)
	ḥꜣt	hat	front of a lion (often writes the word 'front' and related words)
	ḥqꜣ	heqa	king's sceptre (often writes the word 'to rule' and related words)
	ḥtp	hetep	loaf on a mat (often writes the word 'peace' and related words)
	ḫpr	kheper	beetle (often writes the phrase 'to become' and related words)

When you look at Egyptian inscriptions, you'll notice that two- and three-letter signs often have one or two additional signs spelling out the second or third letters. These are called 'phonetic complements'. For example, *htp* is written with a single sign, as , but sometimes also as with the *t* and *p* spelled out to help the reader.

We've looked at about forty hieroglyphs so far. How many of them can you remember, without looking back? They are just a few of the 750 signs that Egyptian scribes had to memorize.

Pictures, Signs and Words

As you saw on pages 14–18, nearly all hieroglyphs are pictures of things. They include figures, animals, natural features such as the sky, and a range of man-made objects. These things look exactly the same in hieroglyphs as they do in Egyptian art. The hieroglyph that writes the word 'tree'  looks the same as pictures of trees in Egyptian paintings and carvings. This painting comes from the tomb-chapel of an official called Nebamun at Thebes about 1360 BC.

19

A tree, shown in a wall-painting of a garden, from the tomb-chapel of Nebamun at Thebes.

Word Signs

You've seen that signs can write a single sound or a group of sounds, but sometimes one hieroglyph can represent a whole word. This use can be quite simple. For example, a hieroglyph showing the ground-plan of a house writes the word for 'house' in Ancient Egyptian. It transliterates as *pr* (say 'per').

You can spot these word signs easily, because Egyptian scribes added a single stroke underneath to mark any picture-sign that wrote a whole word. (They did help their readers, despite what you might think!) So the word for 'house' is usually written . (To find out how to write 'houses', see page 36.)

Sometimes the meanings of these whole-word signs are less obvious. A picture of the sun can write the Ancient Egyptian word for 'sun', *rͨ*, but it also writes the word for 'day', *hrw*. With a bit of thought, you could probably figure out that one sun equals one day, but other words are not so obvious. A good example is the word for 'god' *nṯr* . This is written not with a picture of a god, but with a picture of a flag-pole. Why? Because the ancient Egyptians used flags to mark a god's temple as a sacred space.

Playing with Words

The Egyptians also used word-play in their writing. The Ancient Egyptian words for 'house' and 'go' sounded similar, so the sign for 'house' *pr* ⬜ could also write the word 'go' *pr*.

In the same way, a picture of a duck 🦆 could write the word *s3*, meaning 'son', because *s3t* 'duck' sounded similar in Ancient Egyptian. Look at the duck hieroglyph carefully, because you'll see it again later in a very important phrase that often turns up near the names of Egyptian pharaohs (page 59).

You might think that using the same signs for different words would be confusing, but the Egyptian writers had a clever way to make sure you knew which meaning they were using. If you want to find out what it is, look ahead to page 23.

This word play, based on the sounds of words, is how the twenty-four alphabetic signs (see pages 14–16) got their sound meanings:

a picture of a mouth writes the sound of *r*, because the Ancient Egyptian word for 'mouth' is *r3*.

a picture of a reed writes the sound of *j*, because the Ancient Egyptian word for 'reed' is *j*.

a picture of a pool writes the sound of *š* because the Ancient Egyptian word for 'pool' is *š*.

What Can Hieroglyphs Do?

Hieroglyphic writing is very clever and flexible. The same hieroglyph can be used both as a picture sign and as a sound sign.

In ⟨glyph⟩ the mouth is a picture sign, writing the word *r3* meaning 'mouth'.

In ⟨glyph⟩ it is a sound sign, writing the letter *r* in the word *pr* meaning 'go'.

Sometimes one sign can write a whole word, and it can mean more than one thing (like ⟨glyph⟩ the sign for 'duck' and 'son'). In the next section, you'll find out how the Egyptian scribes helped the reader to work out which meaning was which.

These hieroglyphs read 'Very good!' or 'Well done!' You already know more about hieroglyphs than all the scholars in Europe did before Champollion deciphered the Rosetta Stone.

Picture Clues

You have got the idea that the same hieroglyphic sign can write different meanings. This isn't so different from English – think about the word 'bear'. 'Bear' can be the name of a furry animal, or a verb meaning to carry something, or to put up with something. You can probably think of lots more words like that. But how do you know which meaning is being used? You can work it out from the rest of the sentence. If someone says to you, 'I can't bear this hot weather', or 'I won't go to bed without my bear!', you aren't in any doubt what they mean. But if you just see the word 'bear' by itself, you have no clues to the meaning.

However, the ancient Egyptian scribes did give their readers clues. They put special picture signs at the end of words to help the reader to know what the word was about. We call these picture signs 'determinatives' because they help us determine (work out) what the word means.

The names of the stars, and any words to do with the stars, end with a picture of a star ✩ .

Names of trees, and any words to do with trees, end with a picture of a tree ⍭ .

Determinative signs can also have extended meanings. A picture of a rolled-up papyrus roll ▱⧓▱ , which was the Egyptian equivalent of a book, could write the word for 'roll' *mdꜣt*. But it could also be a signal for words to do with 'writing'. By a further jump, scribes used it to signal words to do with abstract ideas (such as truth, beauty, wisdom) because these ideas might be written down on a papyrus roll.

These are some of the commonest determinatives that you will see in hieroglyphic writing:

Sign	What it shows	What it signals
	seated man	personal names, and words to do with a man, his relationships and occupations
	seated woman	as above, but for a woman
	seated child	as above, but for a child
	a man and woman	words to do with men and women, and people
	a seated god	names of gods, and words to do with gods
	man with hand to mouth	words to do with eating, drinking, speaking, thinking and feeling
	man sitting	words about sitting, relaxation
	man collapsed on the ground	words to do with being tired
	man with a staff	words for officials and other important men
	prisoner	words about prisoners, people who should be prisoners, and enemies
	arm holding a stick	words to do with physical force, effort and strength
	legs walking	words to do with movement

Sign	What it shows	What it signals
𓂻	legs walking backwards	words to do with movement backwards
𓃒	bull	words about bulls, cows and cattle generally
𓅮	sparrow	words to do with little things (because the sparrow is a little bird), and also bad things
𓈉	hill-country	words for hill-country, deserts, foreign places and foreign place names
𓊖	town with cross-roads *(seen from above)*	names of towns, and words to do with towns
𓇅	plant	names of plants and words about plants and vegetation
𓊛	ship	words about ships and travel on the river
𓎞	woven cattle stall	words for woven things
𓏞	papyrus roll	words for book, writing and written things; also for abstract ideas

Determinatives also help the reader to tell similar words apart. The verb 'to write' is *sš* and it is written with a picture sign of a scribe's writing equipment . The same picture is used for 'writing' or 'writer'. You can tell them apart by the determinative signs at the end:

𓏞   *sš*   'writing'

𓏜   *sš*   'writer' (or 'scribe')

These determinative end-signs are essential, because words that have the same consonants can mean very different things. The word written as **nfrt** can mean a 'beautiful woman' or a 'cow'. (You wouldn't want to muddle those two up!) The signs **db** can write the word for 'fig' or 'hippopotamus' – quite a difference. The Egyptians knew which was meant by the picture sign at the end, either a bowl of fruit or a hippo:

Can you tell which is which?

In the Old Kingdom, around 2300 BC, one lady probably regretted these determinative signs when she looked at her husband's tomb-chapel at Giza. She was the wife of Tjetji, the Overseer of the Pyramid of King Chephren, and her name was **dbt** (Debet). She is shown in the carved tomb-chapel as slim and beautiful, but her name is written beside her, and it always ends with the sign of a plump hippopotamus ... (And if you are wondering why there is a 't' before the hippopotamus, look at page 36.)

A relief from the tomb-chapel of Tjetji, showing his wife (to the left) and her small daughter, with her name above them.

27

Determinative signs have another useful purpose. They can show us where many words end. This is particularly useful, because hieroglyphic inscriptions have no spaces between words. Spaces aren't needed if the signs tell you where a word ends. This is part of an inscription we'll meet later (see pages 81–83).

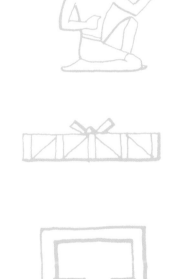

The determinatives also provide us with useful insights into how the Egyptians thought about things and how they grouped things together. You saw on page 24 that the picture group used as the determinative for words such as 'people' shows a seated man and a seated woman . The man always comes first, because in ancient Egyptian society, men were considered to be more important than women.

The word ![glyph] or *j3kb*, meaning 'mourning', has a picture hieroglyph as a determinative. It shows some curls of hair ![glyph]. This was because people in mourning dishevelled their hair. A determinative showing a crocodile ![glyph] is applied to words about crocodiles, but also to various words expressing greed, rage and other crocodile-like emotions. The Egyptians associated bad feelings with these dangerous animals.

Determinatives also give clues to Egyptologists if we don't know what a particular word meant in Ancient Egyptian. For example, the word ![glyph] *tbsw* is known only from one poem, which was written about 1840 BC. (You can see it on page 75.) We can at least tell that the word is a name of a plant, because of its determinative: ![glyph].

What Else Can Hieroglyphic Signs Do?

Many hieroglyphs were used as picture signs and as sound signs. Some were also used as determinatives. For example, the hieroglyph ![glyph] shows a branch of a tree, which is used to write ![glyph] *ḫt*, meaning 'tree'. From that, it can be used to write the sound *ḫt*, as in ![glyph] *nḫt*, meaning 'strong'. It can also be a determinative of words for wood and wooden objects, such as ⬜ 〰 ⤙ *hbny*, meaning 'ebony', which is a type of hard dark African wood. By the way, 'ebony' is one word that we have borrowed from Ancient Egyptian.

You are probably thinking by now that hieroglyphs sound very complicated. Remember that any writing and spelling system can sound difficult when it is described as a set of rules. However, once you get used to it and use it, it can be very simple and easy. The rules of English spelling sound complicated, but every time you learn a few more words, it gets easier.

Two Words

Here are two Ancient Egyptian words that will show you how the script works in practice: 'cat' and 'dog'.

Cat

Egypt has preserved many images of cats, and even mummified cats. They were sacred animals, but many Egyptians kept cats in their houses to get rid of mice and also as pets. The word for 'cat' was *mjw* (pronounced 'miew'), taken from the sound of a cat's miaowing. It is written: ⟦ 𓏏 𓄿 𓃠 ⟧ .

The first sign writes the two letters *mj* (oddly enough, it represents a milk-jug, the word for which was *mr/mj*). A second sign writing *j* helps to spell this out. (It's a special repeated letter called a

A modern Egyptian cat who lives in the ancient temple at Kalabsha.

31

'phonetic complement'.) The third sign provides the next letter **w**. The final sign is a determinative, showing that this is a small feline animal.

This last hieroglyph shows what the Egyptians considered to be the most characteristic pose of a cat. Egyptian artists painted cats sitting in various ways, though not in as many ways as they do in real life. But the hieroglyphic sign always uses this very upright, formal position. The bronze

A bronze statue of a cat, with earrings, dedicated to the goddess Bastet.

statues that ancient Egyptians gave to the cat-goddess Bastet also have this same pose.

Dog

Dogs were also kept in ancient Egypt, for hunting and as pets. The word for 'dog' was _tsm_. This was written with three sound-signs with a picture of a dog as the determinative:

Mayor Djehutyhotep, who governed the province around el-Bersha in about 1835 BC, had a picture of his dog carved on the walls of his tomb. The dog is rather short and dumpy (unlike the elegant dog in the hieroglyph), and probably was not a fast hunting animal. His name is written above him. He is called $^c nḥw$, meaning 'living one' or 'lively one'.

Part of a wall from the tomb-chapel of Mayor Djehutyhotep showing his bodyguards, his carrying chair, and his dog Ankhu.

3. Words and Texts

Up to now we've been looking mostly at individual signs. Now it's time to see how hieroglyphs work together. When you look at Egyptian hieroglyphs on coffins, sculptures, or papyri (the plural of papyrus), you will usually see whole inscriptions – lines and lines of hieroglyphs. In among them you'll recognize some of the signs as old friends from Chapter 2, but this chapter will give you a lot more help in recognizing and understanding what you see. But where do you start?

Which Direction?

Looking at inscriptions, you'll see that hieroglyphs can face either right or left, and can be written in vertical or horizontal lines. So how do you know where to start reading? And which way to read? There's one important clue. Look at the human figures, animals and birds. They almost always face towards the start of the text.

This is part of the coffin of a lady called Tanetaa from around 700 BC. Usually the writing reads from right to left, as on this coffin, so you can

Part of one side of the coffin of Tanetaa with a funerary spell and a picture of the god Horus.

see that the animals and birds face to the right. Read the top signs first. Hieroglyphs are (almost) always written from top to bottom.

One warning, however, about this rule. The hieroglyphs sometimes face backwards on papyri of the so-called *Book of the Dead* – this is a series of spells to help the dead survive in the Afterlife. These papyri were usually written in vertical lines, in pen-drawn hieroglyphs which face right, but the lines are read from left to right. Scribes probably wrote in this special way to show the papyrus contained a secret and sacred text. This papyrus shows how it worked (and you can find out some more about this particular papyrus on page 68).

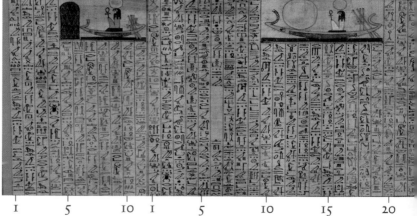

The papyrus of Ani, from his tomb, with spells and illustrations. Line numbers show the order of reading.

I   5   10   I   5   10   15   20

Hieroglyphs were intended to look elegant, and scribes would arrange signs into square groups for the sake of neatness. On a tomb stela (an inscribed slab) from around 1750 BC, the tomb-owner's name is Renefseneb. The signs for his name are written in this order, from right to left:

The stela of Renefseneb
with his relatives offering
food to him.

n r
b s n
f

Scribes had no hesitation in breaking the rules to make their work look beautiful. So, sometimes the signs are arranged slightly out of order, so that they look neater. For example, on another stela the place name Djedu should be written in the order (= *ḏd*+*w*+determinative). However, to make it look more elegant, they actually wrote the signs like this: .

A Few Facts and Figures
Masculine and Feminine

In the Egyptian language, nouns are either feminine or masculine. Female names and nouns always end in *t*, so:

 mjw is 'male cat', but

 mjjt is 'female cat'.

 s is 'man', but *st* is 'woman'.

 s3 is 'son', but *s3t* is 'daughter'.

A **noun** is a word that is a name for a person, a place, a thing or an idea.

Plurals

To make a noun plural in English, you usually add 's' (cat /cats). The ancient Egyptians added *w*. This ending is sometimes spelled out with ℚ *w*, but often a set of three strokes are also added as a determinative to show there is more than one or two of the word 𝍷 𝍷 𝍷. If the noun is feminine, the *w* goes before the *t*. For example, *nfrt* means 'a beautiful woman', but *nfrwt* means 'beautiful women'.

Numbers

Numbers are written like this:

 **1**

 **2**

 **3**

 **4**

 **5**

 **6**

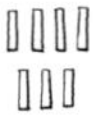 **7**

 **8**

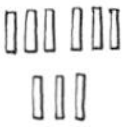 **9**

 **10**

 **20**

 **30** and so on

 **100**

 **1,000**

 **1,000,000**

You will often see the word for 'thousands' on tomb inscriptions. The dead person requests offerings of 'thousands' of various things, including meat, fish, beer, linen (for clothes) and so on (see page 43).

To write numbers in between 10 and 20, or 20 and 30, and so on, signs are put together. So 14 is written with 10 and 4, like this: .

One stela, erected by an official called Ity, is dated to 'Year 14 under the Majesty of the Dual King Kheperkara'. This is another name for Senwosret I, who reigned from 1918 to 1875 BC. So this date works out as 1904 BC.

'Year 14 under the Majesty of the Dual King Kheperkara'

38

Ity

Now try writing out your own age!

Small Words

Many small words are written with just sound-signs and no determinatives. You can spot these words easily with a bit of practice. Here are some of the most common ones:

Sign	Transliteration	Translation
	m	in
	n	for, to, of
	r	towards, against
	$ḥn^c$	together with
	$ḥr$	on

Some Common Words and Phrases

Like any foreign language, Ancient Egyptian can seem very complicated to someone who hasn't grown up learning the language. Even experienced Egyptologists still do not fully understand all the details of Ancient Egyptian grammar. However, there are quite a few common phrases and bits of grammar that you can identify easily on inscriptions with a bit of detective work. Here are some clues for spotting them.

> **Grammar** means the rules for speaking or writing a language.

'Words spoken by'

If you go to Egypt, or look in books about Egyptian temples, you'll see a lot of pictures and hieroglyphs on the temple walls. Many short inscriptions on temple walls are captions to the big pictures. Many of these captions begin with the phrase  _ḏd-mdw jn_, meaning 'words spoken by', and then the name of the person is given. You can see an example in the picture on page 41.

A pillar of a chapel built by
Senwosret I in the temple of
Karnak, about 1890 BC.

41

In this case 'words spoken by' is followed by the name of the god
Atem-Amun, who is shown standing underneath, with King
Senwosret I in front of him.

Place Names

You can pick out place names in inscriptions by finding the
determinative . You'll find it twice in the next inscription in the
place names Djedu and Abydos. (Djedu is in the Nile Delta, and
Abydos is in Middle Egypt. Both these place names turn up fairly
often, because they were cities sacred to Osiris, the god of the dead.)

Osiris, lord of **Djedu**, the great god, lord of **Abydos**

   ḏdw   Djedu

   *3bḏw*   Abydos

42

Offering Prayer

The traditional offering prayer is found on many coffins, stelae and tomb walls. It starts with the group of signs ![signs] .

These read ***ḥtp-dj-njswt***, meaning 'an offering which the king gives'.

This prayer was very old and traditional even then, and so this phrase is written in a very abbreviated way. Most objects that have survived from ancient Egypt come from tombs or chapels, so this group of signs appears a lot on items in museums. It is well worth learning the hieroglyphs for this prayer because you'll be able to find it quite often. The prayer expresses a wish that the king might give an offering to Osiris. Then the god, in his turn, would allow a prayer offering of food to be given to the spirit of the dead man.

ḥtp-dj-njswt wsjr nb ḏdw nṯr ꜥꜣ nb ꜣbḏw

An offering which the king gives to Osiris, lord of Djedu, the great
god, lord of Abydos,

prt-ḥrw tꜣ ḥnqt kꜣ ꜣpd šs mnḫt ḫt nbt nfr wꜥb ꜥnḫt nṯr jm

and a prayer-offering of bread and beer, meat and fowl, alabaster
and linen, everything good and clean which a god lives on.

Look closely at the hieroglyphs in the second line. As you can see,
several of the words are written with picture signs:

Sign	Transliteration	What the sign shows	Meaning
$\bigcirc$	*tꜣ*	loaf of bread	bread
	ḥnqt	jug of beer	beer
	kꜣ	head of an ox	meat
	ꜣpd	head of a bird	fowl or bird

43

4. Places and Contexts

There's another type of hieroglyphic group which appears a lot – names and titles. (The Egyptians were very big on titles.) They are fun and easy to spot. If you want to go straight on and study them, go to page 54. But if you feel you have earned a break from memorizing signs, just sit back and enjoy the hieroglyphs for a while.

Hieroglyphs and Art

Hieroglyphs often appear as part of paintings or carvings. I've said already that scribes took pride in writing their hieroglyphs carefully and elegantly. But the signs could look very different, depending on whether they were drawn with a pen, painted onto papyrus or a tomb wall, or carved in stone.

Remember this sign ? It's the owl that writes the letter *m*. Here are four examples of the sign from four different places in different styles of drawing, carving and painting.

❶ This was carved on a temple doorway in 'raised relief', which means the signs stick out above the surface of the stone.

Part of a temple doorway, built by Amenemhat III for the god Sobek at Medinet el Faiyum.

Part of the stela of an official called Amenemhat (see pages 62–63).

45

② This was carved on a stela in 'sunk relief', which means the signs were cut into the stone.

*From a wall-painting
from the tomb-chapel of
Nebamun at Thebes.*

❸ This was painted on the wall of the tomb-chapel of an official called Nebamun.

❹ This is on a tile from a palace. The sign has been modelled in gold on a blue glazed background.

*A gilded tile from a palace of
Amenhotep III, perhaps
at Thebes.*

Sometimes, these different styles give clues to what sort of person had the text carved. In a chapel that King Senwosret I built in the temple of Karnak around 1890 BC, the signs are carved in beautiful detail showing all the feathers on every bird-sign. Very royal.

47

A detail from a pillar in the chapel of Senwosret I at Karnak.

However, some inscriptions were carved by people who didn't really know what they were doing, and who couldn't afford to employ a skilled scribe or carver, unlike the king. This stela dating from 1750 BC is almost unreadable. The box shows its version of the owl-sign.

A badly carved stela, showing offerings being made to a man. The names are almost unreadable.

205

Hieroglyphic texts were often beautifully mixed with the art on tomb and temple walls. On this stela you can see the offering formula you read on pages 42–43. It is carved above a scene of a man sitting down. The offerings that he had wished for in the prayer are piled up in front of him.

Can you spot the sign for 'thousand'?

The stela of the official Amenemhat (see pages 62–63).

Inscriptions above a scene often tell you the name of someone, or provide a caption telling you what is going on. Here the official Ity (do you remember him from page 38?) is receiving offerings from his sons. The eldest (in front) has the caption 'His son Intef'. The younger son (behind his brother) has the caption 'His son Amenemhat'.

His son Intef

His son Amenemhat

Hieroglyphs can also act as a sort of speech bubble, recording what is being said by the people who are shown in the carvings and paintings. Often these scenes show the servants of the wealthy tomb-owner. Here is a damaged scene from a tomb at Thebes from around 1900 BC. The man is brewing beer from bread, but he is interrupted by a boy demanding food. Notice that the signs in each speech bubble face the same way as the person who is speaking.

This is another scene, this time from the walls of the tomb of the official Ti at Saqqara, around 2500 BC. Here some boatmen are fighting. They are also swearing at each other. What they are calling each other is too rude to translate: 'Come here you *nkw*!'

God's Words

The Egyptians called hieroglyphs *mdw-nṯr*, which means 'god's words', because they believed that the gods had invented writing and that it was sacred. Even so, hieroglyphs were used to write many everyday things, including swear words – as you have just seen!

Thoth, the god of writing, from a wall of the temple of Horus at Edfu.

In religious art, hieroglyphs could act as emblems. Ancient Egyptians wore amulets (lucky charms) in the shape of hieroglyphs. In such a case, the hieroglyph was not just a sound-sign but also a picture of the meaning of the word it usually spelled.

The most common of these signs is , which writes the letters ^cnh (see page 18) – say 'ankh'. This knotted sign shows a piece of clothing, perhaps a sandal strap. It is used to write the words 'to be alive' and 'life'. Gods are shown holding it as a symbol of life. Sometimes the ankhs have arms and are shown as characters in religious and royal scenes. The golden fan of the boy-king Tutankhamun (who reigned around 1332–1322 BC) shows him hunting ostriches in a chariot. An ankh-sign is running along holding a fan over him to keep him cool.

A fan that once had ostrich feathers, from the tomb of Tutankhamun in the Valley of the Kings at Thebes.

Another sign of this sort is . This shows a staff with an animal's head, which was known as the *w3s*-staff. Important officials and gods were shown holding staffs like this as a signal of power.

The sign writes the word 'power' in this common group of hieroglyphs. It reads (from right to left) *ʿnḫ ḏd w3s*, meaning 'life, stability, power' (for the king, of course!). It appears as a piece of decoration on all sorts of royal buildings and objects. The same 'power' sign was also worn as an amulet.

Kings' Names

Kings' names decorate many Egyptian monuments. All stone buildings and monuments were erected by the king or by his officials. Each king had two names and three epithets which were also used as names.

For example, Khakheperra Senwosret II had three other names:

Horus, Leader-of-the-Two-Lands;
Two Ladies, He-Who-Makes-Truth-Appear;
Golden Horus, Grace-of-Gods.

A bronze statue of the god Amun-Ra, holding a w3s-staff and an ankh-sign.

The first two names usually appear in inscriptions – they were the name he was given at birth and the name he took on becoming king. These names were always surrounded by a loop (now called a 'cartouche'). This makes royal names very easy to spot.

A pillar from the chapel built by Senwosret I at Karnak, showing Senwosret offering food to the god Amun-Ra.

55

This is a pillar from the chapel built by King Senwosret I, whose name is written:

Senwosret means 'man (s) of (n) the goddess Wosret'. The 'wosret' part is written first because it is the name of a goddess. Words for gods and kings were placed first in a combination of words because they were considered so important. This did not affect their pronunciation (the king wasn't called Wosret-sen as some early Egyptologists thought!). It is rather like the rule in Egyptian art which means that the most important figures in a scene are shown bigger than everyone else.

A wall-painting showing the official Nebamun hunting birds, from his tomb-chapel at Thebes. His wife, Hatshepsut, is shown much smaller than him.

The most common cartouches in all Egypt are the two names of Ramses II, who reigned from 1279 to 1213 BC. He was a powerful king who extended the Egyptian Empire by war and conquest.

His cartouches are:

A list of kings carved by Ramses II in a temple of Osiris at Abydos.

r^c+wsr+$m\mathfrak{z}^c t$ =
wsr-$m\mathfrak{z}^c t$-r^c =
Wosermaatre
(the r^c is written first because it is the name of the sun god)

r^c+ms+s+s =
Rameses

Each name is accompanied by a description of the king, saying how he was 'chosen by Ra' (the sun god) and 'loved by Amun' (the king of the gods). Ramses II was not exactly the shy retiring type. He erected many buildings and statues for himself, including one of the two huge rock-cut temples at Abu Simbel in Lower Nubia. He even had his name carved onto earlier kings' monuments (see page 64), so his are the best cartouches to learn by heart.

The name of Ramses II on the side of one of the huge statues of the king at his temple at Abu Simbel.

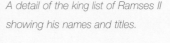

A detail of the king list of Ramses II showing his names and titles.

59

Before the king's birth name (Ramses) comes the title $s3$-r^c 'Son of the sun god' because the Egyptian rulers were believed to be children of the gods. If you look on page 11, you can also see this group on the pillar. You've seen the duck before too, on page 21.

Before the name that Ramses II took when he became king (Wosermaatre) comes the title $nswt$-$bjtj$, meaning 'Dual King'.

The king is also sometimes called ntr-nfr, meaning 'The Good God'.

And also *nb-tʿwj*, meaning 'Lord of the Two Lands' (Upper and Lower Egypt).

After the name often comes a wish for the king to be ⟨figure⟩ *dj-ʿnḫ*, that is 'given life!'.

In some texts, whenever the king or his palace are mentioned, the scribe automatically includes a wish for 'life, prosperity, health' by writing ⟨figure⟩. This is an abbreviation for *ʿnḫ (w)ḏ3 s(nb)*.

Other Names

Non-royal names are harder to spot, but as I said before (see page 24), men's names often end in the determinative ⟨figure⟩, and women's names in ⟨figure⟩. Gods' names often end with a figure of a god ⟨figure⟩ (see page 24), or the flagpole sign ⟨figure⟩ (see page 20). Many objects had their owner's name on them, including objects placed in their tombs. A person's name was very important to keep his or her memory alive.

On tomb inscriptions, the names of the dead are quite easy to find. Often their titles and names follow the description of them as ⟨figure⟩ *jm3ḫ*, meaning 'the blessed one'. *ḫ* spells out the last letter of the sign (it is a 'phonetic complement' – see page 19).

Sometimes the name of the dead person is surrounded by two groups of signs,  and ▱ .

wsjr writes 'Osiris', the name of the god who judged the dead. It is placed before the name of a dead person, so they become 'the Osiris So-and-so'. (As you see, the god's name is often written without a determinative sign.)

The dead person's name is often followed by ▱ *mꜣꜥ-ḥrw*, meaning 'true of voice'. This title is given to those people who have been judged virtuous after their death. (These signs are often placed sideways, for neatness' sake.)

This figure is a 'shabti', a statue that would come to life and act as a servant for its owner in the Afterlife after he had died. It comes from the tomb of 'the priest of Amun, Iwi' who lived around 1730 BC. His name – *jw+w+j* – and title are surrounded by the signs for 'Osiris' and 'true of voice'.

The shabti of Iwi, in the form of a mummy, with a gilded face.

This is the stela of an official named ⸢hieroglyphs⸣ *jmn* + *m* + *ḥȝt* Amenemhat. He is shown sitting in front of a table of offerings. The offering prayer (see pages 42–43) begins in the top line. At the end of the second line comes the phrase 'for the spirit of' – ⸢hieroglyph⸣ *n kȝ n* – which introduces his name and titles. You've met many of the other words and phrases before. The text reads as a whole:

ḥtp-dj-njswt wsir nb ḏdw nṯr ꜥꜣ nb ꜣbḏw

An offering which the king gives to Osiris, lord of Djedu, the great god, lord of Abydos

prt-ḥrw ḥꜣ ḥnqt kꜣ ꜣpdw šs mnḥt ḥt nbt nfr wꜥb ꜥnḥt nṯr jm n kꜣ n

a prayer-offering, bread and beer, meat and fowl, alabaster and linen, everything good and clean which a god lives on for the spirit of

63

jmꜣḥ jmj-rꜣ-ꜥḥnw(tj) jmn-m-ḥꜣt m ꜣꜥ-ḥrw

the blessed one, the Overseer of the Chamber (a courtly title), Amenemhat, true of voice.

The Magic of Hieroglyphs

Monuments had a magic power, because they were intended to ensure a person's future for all time. As we saw on page 58, Ramses II often re-carved inscriptions, putting his name onto monuments erected by an earlier king. This is a piece of a granite temple, where the name of Ramses II has been carved right over the name of King Khakaura Senwosret III, who had lived 600 years earlier.

Part of a temple of Ramses II,
found at Tell Basta.

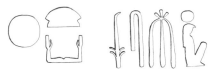

The earlier name reads from left to right $r^c + h^c + k\beta(w) = h^c k\beta(w) r^c$, with the Ra bit placed first as it is the name of the sun god.

The name of Ramses reads from right to left $r^c+ms+s+sw$. You will notice that this is a slightly different spelling of his name than last time.

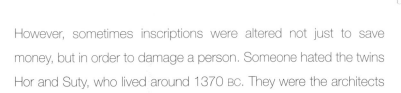

However, sometimes inscriptions were altered not just to save money, but in order to damage a person. Someone hated the twins Hor and Suty, who lived around 1370 BC. They were the architects of the temple of Amun at Luxor.

The ruins of the temple of Amun at Luxor.

Someone has hacked their names and their pictures off their tomb stela. Without their names, their monument was useless.

The granite stela of Hor and Suty, with a detail showing how their names and images have been erased.

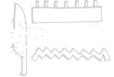

This damage was probably done in the reign of King Akhenaten, who changed the religion of Egypt and even erased the name of the god Amun wherever he found it.

In some very sacred places, such as the king's pyramid or tomb, the hieroglyphs themselves were damaged while they were being carved. This was so that they could not come to life and harm their owner in the Afterlife. In the signs with pictures of humans and animals, the legs or heads were often left off. Sometimes, where the signs showed dangerous creatures, the animals were shown cut up with knives.

On this shabti of an official called Renseneb, who was buried in Abydos around 1730 BC, the birds have no legs, and the figures have nothing from the waist down:

This is how the signs are carved

and how they normally look:

67

The painted stone shabti of the official Renseneb from his tomb at Abydos.

49343

A detail of the papyrus of Ani, illustrating the sun god in his boat. The box shows the name of his enemy, Aapep.

In the papyrus roll of the *Book of the Dead*, made for the King's Scribe Ani around 1280 BC, the name of the evil serpent demon Aapep is written like this ⟶ □ □ ⌇⌇⌇ . The final picture sign (determinative) is a serpent, but you can see that it has knives cutting into its back. (These signs are written with a pen in a vertical line facing right.)

Reading a Text

When we look at an ancient Egyptian text, first we have to transliterate it into a modern alphabet, and then we have to translate the Ancient Egyptian words into English ones before we can actually read it. But you also have to know where and why something was written to understand it properly. Otherwise it is like listening to a football commentary without ever having seen a game. You can understand the words, but without knowing the rules of the game or what it involves, it is impossible to understand what is going on.

For example, the drawing on the right is part of an inscription in the British Museum.

This can be translated as (from top to bottom):
'The Prince and Mayor, Seal-bearer of the King, Sole Friend, Overseer of Priests of Satet the lady of Elephantine, the Mayor Sarenput born of Satethotep, true of voice, lord of blessedness.'

Sarenput

Why was this written? It seems a meaningless string of titles and names.

The inscription is on the bottom half of a statue, now in the British Museum's collection. The Museum acquired it in AD 1887 from Aswan. In the 1980s, the detective work of an American lady Egyptologist, Biri Fay, showed that the Museum also owned the

The bottom fragment of the statue of Sarenput, showing the inscription (on the left).

top half of the statue, which had been acquired earlier, and so they were re-joined.

The two halves of the statue reunited, and Sarenput's face.

The painted niche in the tomb-chapel of Sarenput at Aswan. At the top of the steps you can see the spot where his statue originally sat.

Sarenput's statue is carved out of expensive granite and once had inlaid eyes. It presents him as an important person, with a well-fed body, sitting on a chair. Sarenput is known to have been the mayor of the island town of Elephantine, like his uncle before him, around 1838 BC. His tomb is preserved, high up in the cliffs over the Nile at Aswan. This was an important position, looking down over the island. His statue was placed in a niche at the back of the tomb-chapel, where people would pay their respects to him. You can still see the spot on the floor where it stood.

And so the inscription tells us what was needed for him to be remembered: above all his name, but also his titles. They showed how important he was, and connected him to both the king and to the local goddess Satet. The inscription also includes the name of his mother, Satethotep, who was named after the goddess. Her name means 'Satet is gracious'.

The grand statue with its inscription shows him as wealthy and happy, but we think he died young and suddenly, because his tomb was never finished.

The unfinished outside of the tomb of Sarenput at Aswan, looking down to the island of Elephantine.

5. What Hieroglyphs Tell Us

So far we have looked at hieroglyphs from temples and tombs, which are only part of ancient life. Fully painted hieroglyphs are slow to write and carve, so the Egyptians developed quickly drawn hieroglyphs and then an even quicker style of hieroglyphs now known as 'hieratic'.

Writing Quickly

Simple hieroglyphs drawn with a pen were used for copies of the *Book of the Dead* and other religious texts that were kept in temple libraries or put in people's tombs. They are almost always written from right to left. This is what the word 'cat' looks like in hieroglyphs and in drawn hieroglyphs:

hieroglyphs

drawn hieroglyphs

'Hieratic' writing was so simplified that it is often hard to recognize that the signs came from pictures originally. On page 75 are some signs from a papyrus, written in Thebes around 1800 BC:

Hieratic	Hieroglyphs	Transliteration
		3
		w
or		*m*
		jr
		the man-determinative

This is just like modern handwriting. We can still recognize the hand-writing of some individuals, such as a scribe called Qenherkhepshef. He worked from around 1250 to 1208 BC and he was in charge of the

A papyrus, with The Tale of the Eloquent Peasant, from Thebes.

A papyrus with a letter in Qenherkhepshef's dreadful handwriting.

craftsmen who worked on the tomb of Ramses II and who lived in a village near the Valley of the Kings. He was rather bossy and impatient, and his handwriting was very quick – and very difficult to read.

The flaky limestone of the Theban hills provided a ready source of flakes for writing on.

This joined-up writing, known as hieratic, was used for all sorts of everyday texts, such as business documents, letters and poetry. Qenherkhepshef's village has even preserved many short notes, most of them written on bits of stone from the surrounding hills.

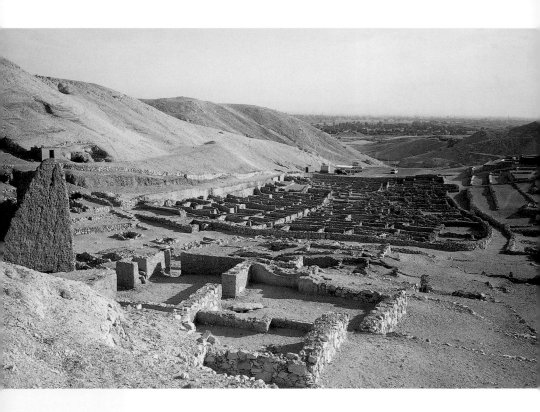

Qenherkhepshef's walled village in the Theban hills, seen from the village cemetery, looking towards the Nile.

One of these notes is a list of who was off work from the work-gang in the Year 40 of Ramses II (1250 BC). We know that one man called Pennub was off one day because 'his mother was ill', while another called Penduauu was off because he was 'drinking with Khonsu'. Their names are written from right to left in a column down the right, with the dates they were off work. Their excuses are written above in red ink. Red ink is often used to highlight certain words. A papyrus tells how these workers went on strike because they had not received their wages on time.

A large flake of limestone from Qenherkhepshef's village, with a list of absences from work.

79

Some of the most famous letters to survive from ancient Egypt were written in the reign of Senwosret I around 1910 BC by a priest called Heqanakht. He lived in the north of Egypt, but worked as a funerary priest at the tomb of the Vizier Ipy at Deir el-Bahri near Thebes. Sitting in a small nearby tomb, he wrote a sequence of letters. He had all the letters ready to give to a messenger to take north, when (it seems) some people arrived to bury someone in the tomb. Heqanakht's letters were accidentally buried in the rubble, and were still there, four thousand years later, when the tomb was excavated in AD 1921 and 1922.

The ruined entrance to Ipy's tomb in the cliffs at Deir el-Bahri. An arrow shows the small tomb where Heqanakht's letters were buried.

The letters are now in the Metropolitan Museum, New York. They are mostly about paying rent, but they also mention a family quarrel between Heqanakht's new wife and his family. This was used by the famous crime writer, Agatha Christie, for her murder mystery, *Death Comes as the End*. In the letters you can see where Heqanakht is changing his mind as he writes, and where he is getting excited and angry, as he writes more quickly.

This is Heqanakht's name:

$$\mathit{ḥq3 + q}$$
$$+ n + \mathit{ḫt} + \mathit{ḫ} + t \qquad = \mathit{ḥq3\,nḫt}$$
$$+$$
determinative

These everyday texts, written in hieratic, are more truthful about what really happened in ancient Egypt than most royal inscriptions. Although many inscriptions survive on temples and tombs, these scribbled documents were the ones that dominated everyday life for everyone who could read and write. Letters, medical textbooks, accounts of deliveries and trade, wills, legal documents, and even stories and love-songs – there was a whole world of different writings.

81

Reading with the Dead

As you have seen, we can never be sure of what a text tells us without knowing why and where it was written. On a stela from around 1880 BC, the official Intef describes himself and his career under King Senwosret I, to encourage people to give him offerings (see pages 42, 72). The stela was placed in a mud-brick chapel, which was close by the temple of Osiris at Abydos which was where Osiris was believed to be buried. The chapel also contained a statue of Intef, showing him as slightly plump – this was to show how wealthy he was.

Each line of the inscription, written vertically, begins with the hieroglyphs  *jnk*, meaning 'I was ...'. One line reads:

The statue and stela of Intef from his chapel at Abydos.

jnk qb šw m ḫȝ ḥ-ḥr

I was cool, free from impatience

(*literally* 'hasty-face')

This is how Intef wanted to be remembered, but of course he may not have been any of these things. Such inscriptions only tell us what the rich people who had them carved wanted us to know. The ancient Egyptians knew this as well as we do – one inscription notes 'every man boasts about himself in his own writings'.

Other types of text sometimes tell us another story, however. *The Tale of Sinuhe* survives in several papyri from the Middle Kingdom. This is one of the great poems from ancient Egypt, and was probably written while Sarenput (see pages 69–73) was alive. It tells us about a man who served Senwosret I, like Intef, but who then ran

The sacred plain at Abydos near where chapels were built (with a modern house built by Egyptologists excavating here).

A hieratic papyrus of The Tale of Sinuhe *being read.*

away from Egypt. He stayed away for many years, and only returned to Egypt in old age, after failing to find a meaningful life abroad. It is written like Intef's stela with its description of a career, but shows us a less ideal person, who is very un-cool. Although it is a made-up description of a life, the poem gives us a feel of the actual experiences and feelings of the ancient Egyptians.

All over Egypt and in museums around the world, many thousands of inscriptions and papyri survive. Many of them have never yet been properly read. Many others have been read, but we don't understand their meaning completely, or their poetry. When we read them, we have to translate them into English, but we must also listen carefully to the ancient writers, and remember how different their world was from ours. They give us another view of the world. Or, as one ancient Egyptian poet wrote:

nfr ḏd n m-ḫt ntf sḏm:f st

'It is good to speak to the future – it will listen.'

6. Writing Hieroglyphs

Egyptologists always have to remember that hieroglyphs were not written by dead mummies, but by living people, like us. If you want to write in hieroglyphs, it is best to copy the hieroglyphs which were drawn with a pen, such as the ones in the funerary papyri.

Write Like an Egyptian

Here is an alphabet for writing English words. These are for writing from right to left, which is how Egyptians always wrote quickly drawn hieroglyphs.

	Quickly drawn hieroglyphs	Hieroglyphs
a		
b		
c		
d		
e		(you can also leave out any e!)

	Quickly drawn hieroglyphs	Hieroglyphs
f		
g		
h	or	or
i		
j		
k		
l		(this is a two-letter sign, rw, which the Egyptians used to write the sound of l)
m		
n		
o		(this is a two-letter sign, $w3$, which the Egyptians used to write the letter o in foreign names)

87

p		
q		
r		
s	or	or
t		
u, v, w		
x (= ks)		
y		
z		

Using this alphabet, you can write your name. Use a thick black felt-tip pen, so that it draws like a rush pen. At the end, add the determinative picture-sign for a male or female name:

or for a man or for a woman.

For example, 'Gabriel' would be written (from right to left):

You can't write proper hieroglyphs without learning Ancient Egyptian, which is rather hard since we have no living ancient Egyptians to teach us. But we can write our own language in the Egyptian script, with some alterations. You can write in English, using the sound-signs shown on pages 14–16. You can also use the determinatives from pages 24–25, or make up suitable new determinatives.

After all, the ancient Egyptians never had to write anything about cars or computers!

In Ancient Egyptian, you would write the sentence 'the cat sat on the mat' like this:

ḥms-mjjt ḥr-tmз (say 'hemes meyet her tema')
sat-cat-on-mat

But you can write 'the cat sat on the mat' as 'th cat sat on th mat' like this, adding determinative picture-signs:

A cat, called Gwen, doing what it says on the papyrus.

Writing Tips

• Modern papyrus paper can be bought in many museum shops or specialist art shops, but you can also use brown wrapping paper.

• Black and red italic felt-tip pens write strokes that look as if they were written with an ancient reed-pen. Use red to highlight important names and words.

• The signs on pages 86–88 can be traced onto thin paper if you have any trouble drawing them at first. The quail chick (the letter *w*) is the worst – if you're not careful, it can often become very blobby. But don't worry – the ancient Egyptians had the same problem ! Have a look at the stela on page 48!

91

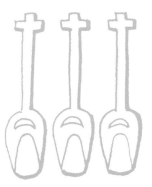

Where to Find Hieroglyphs

The best place to read hieroglyphs is in Egypt, of course, where they cover almost everything. The hieroglyphs in this book are drawn from various monuments, including the chapel of Senwosret I at Karnak (see page 41). I have used thick and thin lines to show whether the sign is in raised relief or sunk relief (see pages 44–45).

Many of the texts in this book come from objects in the British Museum. Each has a number with EA for 'Egyptian Antiquities' (the old name of the Department of Ancient Egypt and Sudan in the museum). The Rosetta Stone, for example, is EA 24, and the stela on page 48 is EA 205. The numbers are useful if you visit the British Museum – they will help you find the right item among the museum's millions of objects. There is a list of the numbers of all the objects shown in this book on page 96. Many of these texts are on display in the Museum's galleries, but some are kept in the storerooms. I have included objects from some of the less-well-known periods of Egyptian history, and also ones where we know their origins. Many other museums in Britain also have Egyptian collections – some of the best are listed on page 93. Visit your local museum, or ask in your local library for more information.

In Great Britain:

The British Museum, Great Russell Street, London

The Ashmolean Museum, Beaumont Street, Oxford

Bolton Museum and Art Gallery, Le Mans Crescent, Bolton

The Egypt Centre, University of Wales, Singleton Park, Swansea

The Fitzwilliam Museum, Trumpington Street, Cambridge

The Liverpool Museum, William Brown Street, Liverpool

The Manchester Museum, University of Manchester, Oxford Road, Manchester

The Oriental Museum, University of Durham, Elvet Hill Road, Durham

The Petrie Museum of Egyptian Archaeology, University College, Market Place, London

93

The Royal Museum of Scotland, Chambers Street, Edinburgh

Famous Egyptian collections in museums around the world include:

The Egyptian Museum, Cairo, Egypt

Brooklyn Museum of Fine Arts, Brooklyn, USA

The Egyptian Museum, Berlin, Germany

The Egyptian Museum, Turin, Italy

The Louvre, Paris, France

Metropolitan Museum of Art, New York, USA

Further Reading

There are many books on hieroglyphs and ancient Egypt. Here are some of the best:

Carol Donoughue,

> *The Mystery of the Hieroglyphs: Egyptian Hieroglyphs and How They Were Deciphered.*
> British Museum Press, 1999.

Geraldine Harris,

> *Gods and Pharaohs from Egyptian Mythology*
> (The World Mythology Series). Peter Bedrick, 1993.

Geraldine Harris,

> *Ancient Egypt* (Cultural Atlas For Young People Series).
> Facts on File, 1990.

Geraldine Harris and Delia Pemberton,

> *British Museum Illustrated Encyclopaedia of Ancient Egypt.*
> British Museum Press, 1999.

Eloise Jarvis McGraw,

> *The Golden Goblet.* Puffin Books, 1986.
> (A good novel set in Qenherkhepshef's village.)

Meredith Hooper,

> *Who Built the Pyramid?* Walker Books, 2001.
> (An imaginative story about the building of Senwosret I's pyramid.)

To learn Ancient Egyptian more fully, the best book is:

Mark Collier and Bill Manley,

>*How to Read Egyptian Hieroglyphs.* British Museum Press,
>1998. (This book is based on objects in the British Museum,
>many of which are also used in this book.)

You could also read:

Jaromir Malek,

>*A B C of Egyptian Hieroglyphs.* Ashmolean Museum, 1994.

Richard Parkinson,

>*Cracking Codes: The Rosetta Stone and Decipherment.*
>British Museum Press, University of California Press,
>1999. (A book about writing in ancient Egypt.)

To try some ancient Egyptian literature:

R.B. Parkinson,

>*The Tale of Sinuhe and other Ancient Egyptian Poems
>1940–1640 BC* (Oxford World's Classics). Oxford University
>Press, 1998.

The numbers of objects in the British Museum, with the pages on which they appear

EA 24	p. 10	1147	p. 32
98	pp. 69–70	5634	p. 78
117	pp. 57, 59	10274	p. 75
157B	p. 27	10683	p. 76
205	p. 48	10470.22	pp. 34, 68
461	pp. 28, 82 (right)	24390	p. 61
581	p. 82 (left)	30360	p. 33
586	pp. 38, 50	37977	p. 58
587	pp. 43, 45, 49, 62–63	37983	p. 19
636	p. 35	37985	p. 46 (top)
826	p. 66	41643	p. 46 (bottom)
1010	pp. 69–70	49343	p. 67
1072	p. 45 (top)	51821	p. 54
1102	p. 64	58517	p. 31